THE
LONELY MONK
AND OTHER PUZZLES

IVAN MORRIS

The Lonely Monk and Other Puzzles

Illustrations by
HUGH CASSON

THE BODLEY HEAD

LONDON SYDNEY

TORONTO

© Ivan Morris 1970
Illustrations © Sir Hugh Casson 1970
ISBN 0 370 01350 6
Printed and bound in Great Britain for
The Bodley Head Ltd
9 Bow Street, London, WC2
by William Clowes & Sons Ltd, Beccles
Set in Monotype Fournier
First published 1970

CONTENTS

For the meaning of *, **, and *** see Preface

Preface 8

1   The Lonely Monk ** 15
2   The Chancellor and the Mafia *** 16
3   The Chess Players ** 17
4   Mr Tabako's Motor-Car * 17
5   Pearls and Jars ** 18
6   Women *** 20
7   Black and Beautiful ** 22
8   Jealous Husbands ** 23
9   Monkeys and Coco-nuts *** 24
10 The Coloured Map ** 25
11 Pints and Tankards ** 26
12 The Loved Ones ** 27
13 Are Some Japanese People Unkind? *** 28
14 A Novelist at Work ** 30
15 On the Kyoto Super-Expressway ** 31
16 A Lady of Fashion and Her Children ** 32
17 Food ** 34
18 The Three Terrorists *** 36

19 Things * 38
20 The Laetitia Riddle * 38
21 The Barrel of Saké * 40
22 Fu Hsi's Eight Diagrams ** 42
23 Odd Men Out ** 42
24 That, And, Had ** 43
25 A Dull Number * 43
26 Angus MacGregor and Professor Baba * 44
27 Three Bankers and Two Fishermen *** 46
28 A Beautiful Chess Problem *** 48
29 Professor Suzuki's Children ** 49
30 Matches * 50
31 Neighbours and Utilities * 51
32 The Three Poachers and Their Punish-
    ment *** 52
33 Bishop Stephen's Nursery * and *** 54
34 Professor Baba's Bet ** 56
35 Animal Words * 56
36 The Scorpion ** 57
37 Casualties of War ** 58
38 The Bishop of Salisbury's Riddle *** 60
39 Mechanical Beetles * 61
40 Missing Words * 62
41 The Vizier's Will * 63

42 Jelly-Beans ** 64
43 English Rebus * and French Rebuses ** 66
44 Chess Clocks * 67
45 General Crackblood and the Courier ** 69
46 The Dishonest Porter * 70
47 A Number Circle and Two Number
   Series ** 71
48 First Night in Paris ** 72
49 Percy's Death * 73
50 Vowels (a)* (b)** 74
51 A Variation of Nim *** 75
52 The Professor's Dinner Party ** 76
53 The Sheik's Camels ** 78
54 Many Numbers ** 80
55 Jock MacKeetch and His Wife ** 81
56 Gaston and the Beer * 82
57 February 1972 ** 84
58 Arnold Toynbee's Grandfather * 84
59 The Balloon ** 85
60 Bombs ** 86
61 Nobel Prizes * 87
62 Transformations ** 88
63 Longfellow's Bees * 88
   Solutions 91

PREFACE

Puzzles breed puzzles, and often the children out-shine their parents. Having recently put together all the best ones I knew (*The Pillow-Book Puzzles*), I never imagined that I would soon have an even richer supply in my larder; but so it is, and here they are.

This second helping comes mainly from ideas suggested to me by friends and correspondents who, having read my first puzzle book, realized I was an addict; others are variations on themes announced in the earlier collection; still others came to me completely out of the blue, usually when I woke up in the middle of the night.

Though I avoid puzzles that depend on special skills or knowledge, I could not resist the temptation to include one of Dawson's beautiful chess problems (a seemingly simple mate in two), and I have also used a couple of amusing, if slightly off-colour, French rebuses. The star system is the same as in my previous collection: * indicates Brief Diversion, ** Hard Nut, and *** Herculean. Readers are bound to disagree about my assessments (many of my Herculeans would no doubt be Brief Diversions for an Einstein), but I think they are useful as rough guides.

Bishop Stephen and young Percy have survived from my earlier cast, but all the other *dramatis personae* are new. Quite a few Japanese people have joined the ranks, possibly because I compiled the collection during a recent stay in Kyoto. Among them are Mr Tabako, an energetic, well-travelled businessman, typical of the New Japan, who loves both his racing-cars and his children, and Professor Baba, a distinguished academic gentleman who ekes out his modest salary with bets and lecture tours. Despite the vast difference in their styles of life, they are close friends and used to be neighbours.

Puzzles, I have found, admit no national boundaries: unlike humour, they are a sort of Esperanto of the mind. Even the best English joke or anecdote falls flat in Osaka, whereas a good puzzle is a truly international coin, giving equal pleasure to the happy few wherever they may be.

From the publication of my previous puzzle book I learnt that far more people enjoy these mystifications than I had supposed. Many acquaintances whom I would never have suspected of such tastes proved to be obdurate solvers. But reactions varied. The least enthusiastic was from a friend who confessed not only that he had failed to enjoy the puzzles but that the very sight of the book inspired him with nausea. Among the many judicious corrections that I received from a host of fellow-addicts scattered round the world from Glasgow to Hawaii was one about the two Abyssinians who enter a bar, one being the father of the other's son. In my answer to this Brief Diversion, which I learnt during my distant days in preparatory school, I naively stated that they were husband and wife. 'It is refreshing', writes my learned correspondent, 'to find that there are still people who refer to a couple who have participated in the conception of a child as husband and wife. But the pedant must insist that the answer is incomplete.' O tempora! O mores!

Even the keenest puzzler is liable to dark moments when it occurs to him that there may be better ways to use his hours and wits than in trying to solve puzzles, let alone invent new ones. At such times of acedia it is well to remember the words of Dudeney, probably the greatest puzzle-maker of any age. He points out the practical value of these seemingly gratuitous efforts:

> I do hold that the study of such crafty matters is good, not only for the pleasure that is created thereby, but because a man may never be sure that in some sudden and untoward difficulty that may

beset him in passing through this life of ours such strange learning may not serve his ends greatly, and, mayhap, help him out of many difficulties.

Admittedly not all the situations in these puzzles are likely to occur as we pass through this life of ours: few of us will ever be obliged to distinguish between Finnish and Faroese fishermen, and fewer still will have to identify a pile of plutonium bombs on a station platform. But puzzles can have a value far more subtle and profound than the merely practical. Again it is Dudeney who has best expressed it:

Let these matters serve to call to mind the lesson that our fleeting life is rounded and beset with enigmas. Whence we came and whither we go be riddles, and albeit such as these we may never bring within our understanding, yet there be many others with which we and they that do come after us will ever strive for the answer. Whether success do attend or do not attend our labour, it is well that we make the attempt; for truly it is good and honourable to train the mind, and the wit, and the fancy of man, for out of such doth issue all manner of good in ways unforeseen for them that do come after us.

I have occasionally been asked what qualities are most important for solving puzzles. No doubt a modicum of intelligence is helpful; and for all but the most mechanical puzzles one needs a dash of imagination to lead one to the breakthrough. But not less important in my opinion is a combination of obstinacy and optimism which will provide one with the necessary determination to find the right path and buoyant confidence in following it. If one is convinced that the answer will be found, one is already half-way there.

Once again my thanks are due to Sir Hugh Casson for bringing the puzzles alive by his drawings. I am also most grateful to Dr Harry Hazard and Mr Lawrence Latto for all their valuable suggestions.

THE
LONELY MONK
AND OTHER PUZZLES

1

The Lonely Monk

* *

Father O'Sullivan, a young Zen monk, leaves his mountain hermitage at 5 a.m. and walks rapidly down the narrow path to the nearest village. He arrives before sunset and stays at a temple. After a few days he starts back up the mountain at 5 a.m., but since the path is steep and he is carrying a large box of pickled radishes his speed on the return journey is somewhat less than on the descent. He stops a couple of times for a short rest; at one of these stops he hears the distant booming of a temple bell and knows it will be dark by the time he reaches his hermitage. He also realizes that he passed this very point at exactly the same time of the day on his way down. As he continues trudging up the mountain it occurs to him with a flash of *satori*-like illumination that this was no mere coincidence but was bound to happen at some point on his way.
Is he correct? And, if so, why? Or, if not, why not?

(Based on an idea of Arthur Koestler's)

2

The Chancellor and the Mafia

* * *

A hundred undergraduates are seated in the Assembly Hall. Ninety-nine of them are consistently honest or consistently dishonest, while one of them sometimes lies and sometimes tells the truth. The Chancellor, who knows this but has no idea which students tell the truth and which don't and which one equivocates, is allowed a total of two questions to discover whether the recent drug traffic in the university is under the control of the Mafia. All the students know the answer. What are the Chancellor's questions?

(Adapted from a suggestion by Robert Cupples, Esq., Queen Margaret Hall, Glasgow)

3

The Chess Players

* *

Jock MacKeetch, his sister, his son, and his daughter all play chess. The best player's twin and the worst player are of opposite sex; the best player and the worst player are of the same age. Who plays the best game of chess?

(Offered by Michael Knibbs, Esq.)

4

Mr Tabako's Motor-Car

*

Mr Tabako drives his Honda-Superspeed car round a one-mile circular track at 30 m.p.h. At what speed must he travel on his second lap in order to average 60 m.p.h. for the two laps?

(Contributed by Professor Paul Varley)

5

Pearls and Jars

* *

Mrs Tabako has fifty natural pearls, fifty cultured pearls, and two Ming jars. If she uses all the pearls, how should she distribute them in the two jars in such a way that when Mr Tabako enters the room and picks one pearl out of either jar at random he will have the best possible chance of picking a cultured pearl? What is the distribution and what are his chances?

(Adapted from a puzzle posed by 'Doc' Hume)

Supplementary: What distribution would produce the *least* possible chance of picking a cultured pearl?

6

Women

* * *

What conclusion can be drawn from the following six premises:

(a) all women who play the French horn before breakfast have a chance of becoming creative artists of no mean stature;

(b) Prunella van Blitz has a small waist and absurdly large breasts;

(c) no women who make sweet, docile wives drink alcoholic beverages;

(d) no women who are teetotallers fail to prefer smoking cigarettes to committing adultery in the afternoon;

(e) women who don't play the French horn before breakfast make sweet, docile wives;

(f) no women with small waists and absurdly large breasts prefer smoking cigarettes to committing adultery in the afternoon.

Prunella van Blitz

7

Black and Beautiful

* *

Prove that BLACK is not the square root of BEAUTIFUL.

(Algorithm invented by Dr Harry Hazard)

8

Jealous Husbands

* *

Three jealous husbands with their wives wish to cross a river at a ferry. They find a boat without a boatman, but the boat is so small that it can contain no more than two of them at once. How can these six people cross the river so that none of the women is left with any of the men unless her husband is present? Only three of the six people can row the boat, and men must row rather than women if a choice is possible.

(Translated from Problèmes plaisants et délectables *by Claude-Gaspar Bachet, Sieur de Méziriac, Lyons, 1612)*

9

Monkeys and Coco-nuts

* * *

There are five men and one monkey and a pile of coco-nuts on a desert island. One man goes to the pile of nuts, gives one to the monkey, removes a fifth of the remaining nuts, buries them and goes to sleep. The second man then wakes up, goes to the pile of coco-nuts, gives one to the monkey, buries a fifth of what remains, and goes to sleep. The other men do likewise. In due course all five men wake up and go over to the pile of coco-nuts, which they then succeed in sharing equally among them. What is the smallest possible number of coco-nuts that the pile originally contained?

(Transmitted by Gillon Aitken, Esq.)

Supplementary (propounded by Martin Gardner, Esq.):
If after the final division there is still one coco-nut left for the monkey, what is the smallest possible number in the original pile?

10

The Coloured Map

* *

Miss Tabako wishes to colour a sketch map of old Japan which is divided into 68 provinces. She wants to colour the map in such a way that no two neighbouring provinces have the same colour. Her father gives her some crayons. 'But there aren't enough,' she says. 'Oh yes, there are,' replies Mr Tabako. 'With these crayons you could colour a map with any number of provinces without ever using the same colour for two neighbouring provinces.' How many crayons did he give her?

(Based on an offering by Vercors)

11

Pints and Tankards

* *

Gaston has ten litres of ale in his great cask; his two great tankards (5-litres and 3-litres) are empty. Using no other article, with no marking on any of the three vessels, and not wasting a single drop of ale, how does he put exactly one litre in each of his tankards? (Hint: drinking ale is not a waste.)

12

The Loved Ones

* *

'The loved ones', as they were called in the fashion-
able suburb where they all lived, consisted of the
doctor and his wife, six other young married couples,
three merry widows, twelve dashing bachelors, ten
unmarried girls, and Percy Cod. In the course of a
single month every member of this group except
Mr Cod had sexual relations once with every other
member, with the following exceptions and addi-
tions: there were no homosexual relations between
the men; no married man had relations with any
married woman except his own wife; all the bachelors made love to each of the unmarried girls
exactly twice; the widows had no sexual relations
with each other; and Percy Cod made love to no
one. What was the total number of sexual relations
among members of the group during the month?

*(Based on a puzzle by H. E. Dudeney, and inspired by
John Updike's novel,* Couples)

Supplementary (suggested by Dr Harry Hazard):
Which sub-group *(e.g.* bachelors, widows) had the
highest *per capita* score, and how high was it?

13

Are Some Japanese People Unkind?

* * *

'Like so many Japanese these days,' said Professor Baba to his colleague, Professor Suzuki, 'you are quite a tall man, and tall people are inscrutable.' 'Yes,' said Suzuki. 'And generous people are always scrutable, aren't they?' 'Quite so,' replied Baba. 'And by the same token honest people are invariably generous. . . . By the way, I have recently decided that kind people are always honest.' 'I see,' said Suzuki. 'Then presumably we can conclude that there is such a thing as an unkind Japanese.'

Does Professor Suzuki's conclusion follow logically from the premises in this conversation? If not, what further premise is needed to justify it? And does his conclusion tell us anything about his own nature?

14

A Novelist at Work

* *

Frank Conroy, the author, is writing. His daily output is in proportion to the number of pages that remain to be written: the less that remains, the slower he goes. (According to the inner clock that determines Conroy's speed, a fraction of a page counts as a full page.) If page one takes him 10 days to write and the final page takes 50 days, how many pages are there in the volume and how long will it take him to finish?

(Based on an idea suggested to me by Frank Conroy)

15

On the Kyoto Super-Expressway

* *

Motoring along the super-expressway between Kyoto and Bingo, Mr Tabako sees exactly 100 cars coming in the opposite direction; they, and all the cars behind them, are travelling at the prescribed speed of 50 m.p.h. (as is Mr Tabako) and he sees them at equal intervals of time. If, instead of motoring to Bingo, Mr Tabako had parked his car at the entrance to the super-expressway in Kyoto without in any way affecting the Bingo–Kyoto traffic, how many cars would he have seen coming towards him along the expressway during the length of time it actually took him to reach Bingo?

(Introduced by Mr Keiji Uenishi)

16

A Lady of Fashion
and Her Children

* *

A lady of fashion, who is sometimes described as belonging to the 'jet set', has six children, three girls and three boys. Their birthdays fall in only three months of the year, and they were all born in a period of almost exactly a dozen years. Each of the three birthday months contains the birthdays of a boy and a girl. If we divide the children into three pairs (eldest boy and girl, middle boy and girl, youngest boy and girl), we find that while only one of these pairs consists of children with birthdays exactly two years apart, nevertheless for half the year the ages of the children in the other two pairs, when given to the press (which the lady of fashion is naturally fond of doing), sound quite genuinely as if the boy and girl in each pair had been born at two-yearly intervals if you merely give the ages without the months, though in fact the intervals are greater. All four children in these two other pairs have birthday-months with the same initial letter. The youngest of the six children was born in February of a year whose second digit is the sum of the first and last digits and the same as the third digit read upside down. In what month and year was the second eldest child born?

(Adapted from an invention offered to me by Lady Antonia Fraser)

17

Food

* *

Each of these six passages has twenty words and each concerns food. Pair them into groups of two, explaining what characterizes each group. The characteristics relate to the words, not to the content.

(a) 'Bat soup,' said Major Hogg, 'is hardly a dish most of us long for, but in fact it's surprisingly tasty.'

(b) My very best recipe for cooking foxes was given to me when we were staying with Belinda's grandmother near Bognor.

(c) I well remember how after the absurdly short shooting season old Mac and I eagerly started on our pet rabbits.

(d) 'Oh, awful, awful!' exclaimed Alice. 'Oh, unfortunate elephants. Uncle Ernest is attacking and eating all our old ones in October.'

(e) Attitudes to food in America are based on Puritanism and memories of the frontier; that is why it's so awful.

(f) When we began stewing the electrician's elbow,

Percy objected strenuously. 'Please desist. Even
we have never eaten *live* people before.'

Bat soup

18

The Three Terrorists

* * *

Algernon, Basil, and Cyril have been arrested on suspicion of 'terrorist' activities and a Special Military Tribunal under General Crackblood has decreed that two of the three men will be shot on the following day. Until then each of them is kept in solitary confinement. Algernon has a chat with the gaoler, who knows which two of the men are to die. 'I realize that at least one of the two others is going to be executed,' says Algernon. 'Who is it? My own fate won't be changed in the slightest if you tell me whether it is Basil or Cyril who is going to die.' 'Not so,' replies the gaoler after some deep thought. 'If I were to inform you that Basil was definitely going to be shot, or alternatively that Cyril was

doomed, your chances of survival as you see them would improve considerably.' Who is correct, Algernon, or the gaoler, or neither? Why?

(Provided by Professor S. Devons)

Supplementary (invented by Martin Gardner, Esq.): Suppose that the gaoler in fact told Algernon that Basil was to die. Algernon has a secret way of communicating with Cyril by tapping on the wall of his cell, and he informs him that Basil is doomed and that they therefore both have a 50-50 chance of survival. If Cyril is a brilliant logician, what conclusion will he draw from the news about Basil?

19

Things

*

(a) What food appears more voluminous *after* a meal than before? *(Suggested by Nobuko Morris)*

(b) What vehicle normally moves independently and in a completely different direction within another moving vehicle? *(ibid)*

(c) What creature can become at least a thousand times more valuable when ill than when in good health?

20

The Laetitia Riddle

*

Laetitia has a large one
And so has Cousin Luce;
Eliza has a little one,
But big enough for use.

Each child has a little one
Enclosed within a clout;
In fact all females have one—
No girls are born without.

Hermaphrodites have none;
Mermaids are minus, too;
Nell Gwyn possessed a double share,
If all we read be true.

Lasciviousness there has its source;
Harlots its use apply.
Without it lust has never been,
And even love would die.

'Tis known to all in nuptial bliss,
In carnal pleasure found.
Without it love becomes extinct—
The word is but a sound.

Now tell me what my object is,
But pause before you guess it;
If you be mother, mate, or man,
I swear you don't possess it.

21

The Barrel of Saké

*

Two brothers, Kichibei and Magoichi, own a little inn on the old Great Eastern Highway. One day they are returning to their inn with a barrel full of *saké*. They have agreed not to drink any of the *saké* themselves, since it is all intended for their customers; but Kichibei becomes unbearably thirsty and, taking a silver coin from his purse, offers it to Magoichi in return for a large ladleful of *saké*. Magoichi agrees to the sale. Seeing his brother drink, he himself becomes thirsty and offers the same coin in return for a similar drink. Once they have started, they find it hard to stop, and the coin changes hands time after time until the barrel is empty. Kichibei is much dismayed, but Magoichi comforts him by pointing out that they have had the pleasure of drinking an entire barrel of *saké* for the price of a single silver coin. Is Magoichi mistaken in believing that this is a bargain? If so, why?

22

Fu Hsi's Eight Diagrams

* *

In the Eight Diagrams of Fu Hsi (c.3000 B.C.) ☳
is equivalent to our 6, ☷ to our 1, and ☴ to
our 3. What does ☶ represent?

23

Odd Men Out

* *

Identify the 'odd men out' among these anagrams:

(a)	(b)	(c)
Rot Tin Lean	Tan doe	Taps mise
Pus Mire Vio	Get not	Ill nag
Limp Cab Cee	Ret ilk	Sef roe
Pint Ride	Rod are laid	Dec dens
Nine Tits Rang	Iron lented	O Ivan Pill
Posh Lean Biti	Ruse up	O rut pus

24

That, And, Had

* *

Give complete English sentences in which (a) the word 'that', (b) the word 'and' appear five times in succession, and (c) in which the word 'had' appears eleven times in succession.

25

A Dull Number

*

The British mathematician G. H. Hardy called on his friend Srinivara Ramanujan, the Indian mathematical genius, in a taxi with the number 1729. 'That is a dull number,' remarked Hardy. 'No,' replied Ramanujan immediately, 'it is a very interesting number. It is the smallest number expressible as the sum of two cubes in two different ways.' What are the two ways?

(True story supplied by John Train, Esq.)

26

Angus MacGregor and
Professor Baba

*

(a) Angus MacGregor's office is on the 35th floor
of the Royal Insurance Company. Almost every
morning he takes the lift to the 25th floor and
walks up the remaining ten flights of stairs; but
in the evenings he travels all the way down in
the lift from the 35th floor. Why? (Note:
MacGregor has no need or desire for exercise.)

(b) Professor Baba is on one of his lecture tours in Kyushu. Late at night he telephones the room next to his in the hotel. A man answers.

'Is that Mr Tabako?' asks Baba.

'No,' says the man.

Professor Baba puts the telephone down and shortly afterwards (as a result of the telephone call) goes to sleep. Explain his behaviour in four simple words.

27

Three Bankers
and Two Fishermen

* * *

(a) You are confronted with three bankers, one
from Albania, one from America, and one from
Austria. You do not know which is which, but
you do know that one always tells the truth, a
second always lies, and a third sometimes lies
and sometimes tells the truth. How many
questions are needed to identify their respective
nationalities?

(b) On the following day you are confronted with two fishermen, one Finnish and one Faroese, one of whom always tells the truth while the other usually tells the truth but occasionally lies. How many questions do you need to determine their nationalities?

(Based on variations by Professor Herschel Webb)

28

A Beautiful Chess Problem

* * *

White to play and mate in two moves. Explain why there is one *and only one* solution.

(T. R. Dawson invented this magnificent problem)

29

Professor Suzuki's Children

* *

Professors Suzuki and Baba meet in the Dining Hall of Waseda University.

Suzuki: Hullo. How are you this evening?

Baba: Splendid, thank you. And you?

Suzuki: Very well. You know I have three children now.

Baba: Really? How old would they be?

Suzuki: Well, you're good at mathematics and logic. You should be able to work it out. The product of their ages is 36 and the sum of their ages is the same as the number of that house in Osaka you used to live in.

Baba: (after a pause) That is not enough information.

Suzuki: Quite right. Well, the oldest one looks exactly like me.

Baba: Ah, now I can tell their ages.

How old are the three children?

(Suggested by Barry Polsky, Esq.)

30

Matches

*

(a) A dozen matches are arranged in the following pattern:

Move two of them in such a way that you produce seven squares.

(b) Move three of these equal matches to make eight equilateral triangles:

31

Neighbours and Utilities

*

Professor Baba, Mr Tabako, and Percy Cod used to be neighbours. How could you connect water, gas, and electricity to each of their three houses in such a way that none of the pipes crosses another at any point?

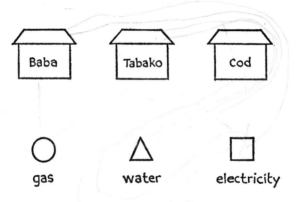

32

The Three Poachers and Their Punishment

* * *

A poacher is detected among the royal elephant herds and brought before the king, a sportsman who detests poachers. His Majesty recalls that he has held two earlier captives in his dungeons for several months, and decides to dispense rough justice. The latest addition, Casimir, is a crack shot who never misses, but solitary confinement on bread and water has so impaired Bertram's skill that he kills only half the time now, while poor Alfonso can kill only one target in every three. So the king gives each his rifle, chains them by the waist to three posts at the corners of an equilateral triangle, and tells them that they will shoot at each other until only one survives, to be released to spread the word of the king's severity, magnanimity, and sporting outlook. To equalize their chances, Alfonso is given first shot, then Bertram, and then the infallible Casimir, with subsequent rounds in the same rotation. If each follows his best strategy in choosing targets, what are the chances of each man to survive the ordeal?

(Suggested by Dr Harry Hazard)

Supplementary: If the king wished to equalize the survival chances of the three poachers by ordering that an equal number of blank cartridges, indistinguishable from the real ones, be mixed into one or more men's ammunition, how many such blank cartridges would be distributed and to whom?

33

Bishop Stephen's Nursery

*

and

* * *

Bishop Stephen buys a nursery of fruit trees en bloc. It consists of a number of trees laid out in rows with the same number of trees in each row as there are rows. There are ten poor priests in his diocese and he generously gives the same number of trees to each priest. When the gifts have all been made, Bishop Stephen discovers to his chagrin that only a single tree is left for himself. All the priests plant the trees they have received in square patterns. How many trees did Bishop Stephen start with?

Supplementary: How many trees did the Bishop start with if there were thirteen (instead of ten) poor priests in the diocese?

(Inspired by Michael Knibbs, Esq.)

34

Professor Baba's Bet

* *

To eke out his meagre salary Professor Baba starts offering bets as follows: 'I bet that at least two people in this room have birthdays in the same season.' How many people must be in the room for Baba's chances of winning to be better than even? (It may be assumed that the distribution of birthdays is unaffected by the difference in the lengths of the seasons, *e.g.* that just as many people are likely to have been born in Spring as in Winter.)

35

Animal Words

*

In fifteen minutes write down as many words as possible in the following category: cocky, mulish, capricious, lousy. What quality, apart from being related to animals and being used to describe human beings, is shared by the overwhelming majority of the adjectives?

36

The Scorpion

* *

A room is 30 feet long, 12 feet high, and 12 feet wide. In the middle of the square side in the north of the room, one foot under the ceiling, sits a large scorpion which can only crawl but neither fly nor drop. For some peculiar reason the scorpion wants to crawl the shortest way to a spot which is one foot above the floor in the middle of the opposite (*i.e.* the south) side. How many feet is its shortest route?

(Received from Dr Walter Bergmann)

37

Casualties of War

* *

When visiting a field hospital shortly after an unsuccessful battle General Crackblood is told that precisely two-thirds of the men have lost an eye, three-quarters an arm, and four-fifths a leg. 'It follows', says the General to his aide-de-camp, 'that at least twenty-six of these men must have lost all

three—an eye, an arm, and a leg.' If General Crackblood is correct (and he is), exactly how many men are in the hospital?

(Based on an invention by H. E. Dudeney)

38

The Bishop of Salisbury's Riddle

* * *

This is the famous Bishop of Salisbury's Riddle (also known as Hallam's Enigma), but I have added the last couplet in order to remove ambiguities:

I sit on the rock, and call for the wind,
But the storm once abated, I'm gentle and kind.
I have kings at my feet who await but my nod
To lie down in the dust on the ground where I've
    trod.
I'm oft seen in the world, though known to but few;
The Gentiles despise me, I'm pork to the Jew.
I never passed but one night in the dark
And that was with Noah alone in the Ark.
My weight is three pounds, my length is a mile
And when you have guessed me you'll say with a
    smile
That my first and my last is the boast of our Isle.

A mere nothing I am, yet without me, I vow,
You'll be dead in a trice—you'd be dead even now.

The answer is a word of one syllable.

39

Mechanical Beetles

*

Six mechanical beetles are arranged as follows:

The beetles can jump over each other or move straight forward; but they cannot go backwards, turn round, or move to either side. What is the smallest number of jumping or moving operations necessary for the beetles to end up in this position:

40

Missing Words

*

Supply the missing words in these palindromes:

(a) (question asked in the house of a famous poet in London:) 'Was it – – – – – toilet I saw?'
(b) (apocryphal remark by Henry Purcell:) 'Egad, a base tone – – – – – – – a bad age.'
(c) (advertisement in *The Times Educational Supplement*): 'Note: Nine – – – – – open in Eton.'

41

The Vizier's Will

*

On his deathbed the Grand Vizier, who has two sons, announces that his entire fortune will go to the son whose horse loses a race in which the two of them must compete simultaneously. The sons, both keen horsemen, are accustomed to winning races but do not know how to lose them. Since in this case both are determined to lose, they do not see how such a race is possible, but a wise man explains how it can be managed. What simple method does he suggest?

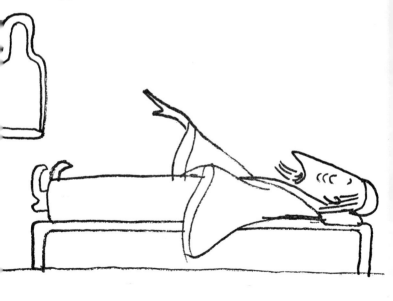

42

Jelly-Beans

* *

Mr Tabako comes home with a box of jelly-beans to be divided among his seven daughters, who are all of different ages. Each girl is to receive from the box the number of sweets by which her age can be divided into the total number of jelly-beans, and all the jelly-beans are to be distributed. Nonchan, who is the middle child if the children are listed in order of their ages, receives 18 jelly-beans. How many years older is she than the youngest girl?

(Based on an idea contributed by Gillon Aitken, Esq.)

43

English Rebus
and French Rebuses

*

(a) English rebus:
   if the B mt put:
   if the B. putting:

* *

French rebuses *(provided by John Napper, Esq.)*:

(b)

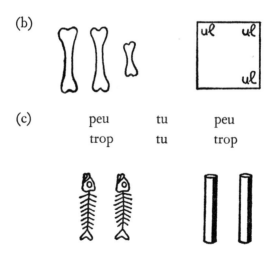

(c)   peu   tu   peu
         trop   tu   trop

44

Chess Clocks

*

Chess clocks have two faces; as soon as a player has completed his move he punches a button which stops his side of the clock and starts his opponent's side; and in this way it is possible at any moment to tell the total amount of time that each player has taken for all his moves. What would be the minimum number of such double-faced clocks required to determine the total time that each of four Scrabble players has taken for all his moves?

45

General Crackblood
and the Courier

* *

A column of men is marching slowly forward at
exactly one mile an hour. General Crackblood, who
is at the rear of the column, tells the courier that he
has a message for the Colonel, who is at the head
of the column ten miles away. 'I want you back here
in exactly one hour,' he says, 'and I want you to go
at an even pace both ways.' Assuming that no time
is lost in actually delivering the message, at what
speed should the courier set off? (It must be re-
membered that by the time the courier reaches the
head of the column it will have moved ahead considerably from its present position.)

(Based on a puzzle posed by John Train, Esq.)

46

The Dishonest Porter

*

Mr Tabako and two business associates arrive at a hotel in St Louis and pay $10 each (a total of $30) for a room, which they intend to share. The manager later decides that he has overcharged them (since the lavatory is not working) and therefore gives $5 to the porter to return to the men. On his way up to their room the porter pockets $2 and returns $1 to each of the men. Mr Tabako and his associates have now paid $9 each (a total of $27); the porter has $2. This makes a total of $29. What has happened to the remaining dollar?

47

A Number Circle and Two Number Series

* *

(a) What is the missing number in the following diagram (based on an advertisement by Aquascutum of London):

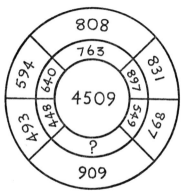

(b) What mathematical property is shared by 60, 65, and 95 but by no other number less than 100? What is the next number in the series?

(Offered by E. J. Ulrich, Esq.)

(c) What is the next number in this series:
$1^1 \ldots 2^2 \ldots 3^2 \ldots 4^2 \ldots 3^3 \ldots$?

48

First Night in Paris

* *

On their first night in Paris Mr Suzuki and Mr Tabako take their wives to an expensive dinner at La Pérouse. Unfortunately Mrs Kazuko Tabako is a teetotaller and Mrs Suzuki has a bad case of diarrhoea. The men agree to 'go Dutch', but Tabako actually pays the bill.

'How much do I owe you?' asks Suzuki on the following morning. 'A few hundred francs,' replies Tabako. 'After all that wine I can't remember the exact amount, but I do recall that the tip I gave the waiter was exactly 20% of the bill (including the wine) and that the sum of the digits in my tip was 20% of the digits in the bill itself.' 'Incidentally, how much did they charge us for that delicious Chambertin?' 'Again I can't recall the exact figure,' replied Tabako. 'But I know it cost precisely one third as much as the food.' 'Well, since your wife didn't drink a drop,' says Suzuki, 'I should pay twice as much for the wine as you do.' 'Fair enough,' says Tabako. 'But by the same token, since your wife didn't eat a morsel, I should pay twice as much for the food as you do.' 'Agreed,' says Suzuki, extracting his wallet. How much should he give Tabako for his share and his wife's?

Supplementary: Why is it usually easier to remember the amount of the tip than the amount of the actual bill?

49
Percy's Death

*

Percy, who comes from a remarkably vigorous family, was born in 1961, the very year in which his father died at the age of eighty. Until what age must Percy live if the year of his death is to share the remarkable property that both the year of his birth and the year of his father's birth have in common?

50

Vowels

*

(a) What English words contain the five vowels, a-e-i-o-u, once and once only in their alphabetical order?

* *

(b) What English words contain them once and once only in the reverse order?

51

A Variation of Nim

* * *

In a variation of Nim, the ancient Chinese stick game, each of two players in turn removes as many sticks as he wishes from either a single pile or two different piles. (He may, for example, remove all the sticks from two piles or just a single stick from one pile.) The player who takes all but one of the sticks from the table wins. How many sticks should you remove from which pile or piles in the following arrangement in order to win?

I II III IIII IIIII IIIIII IIIIIII

52

The Professor's Dinner Party

* *

The Professor and his wife have invited ten people
to dinner, and they are to be seated at a long rec-
tangular table. 'Strange!' remarks the Professor's
wife. 'Precisely half the people at the table will be
Japanese. Can you arrange them so that no Japanese
will be seated next to a non-Japanese (the language
difficulty, you know!), that you and I will be
directly opposite each other, that no two women
will sit next to each other, and that I shall have a
Japanese on one side of me but not on the other?'
'Certainly, my dear,' replies the Professor. 'Nothing
could be simpler. I'll put you next to the Colonel,
and I'll seat old Professor Morris on my right.'
Draw a chart showing the *placement*.

53

The Sheik's Camels

* *

In his Last Will and Testament the Sheik says that anything not specifically bequeathed to a member of his family shall go to the Great Mosque. In the clause concerning his camels he makes the following provisions: 'My eldest son will get half my camels, my middle son will get one third, and my youngest son one ninth.'

Since there are seventeen camels, the sons do not know how to divide them without cutting one of the camels into pieces. While they are discussing the difficulty, a wise man (the same one as in number 41) appears on a camel. The sons ask him what they should do. 'Quite simple,' he says. 'Let us add my camel to yours. There are then eighteen camels, so the eldest of you will get nine, the second will get six, and the youngest two, which makes a total of seventeen, precisely the number that the Sheik left you.' The sons divide the seventeen camels accordingly, and the wise man rides off on his own camel. Is this arrangement satisfactory from everyone's point of view? If not, why not?

54

Many Numbers

* *

(a) addition. What does *money* come to in figures:

SEND
+ MORE
———
MONEY

(b) multiplication. What is a:

27
x   a
————
10b,000,000

(c) multiplication. E = even, O = odd, and there are three possible solutions:

EEO
x   OO
———
EOEO
EEO
————
OOOOO (product)

55

Jock MacKeetch and His Wife

* *

Jock MacKeetch takes a train to arrive home at six o'clock every night; his wife meets him by car and drives him home. One night he was able to leave his office early and took the train an hour earlier than usual. He sent a message to his wife, but she did not get it. Seeing no one at the station, he started walking until he saw his wife coming to fetch him. She saw him and drove him home, and he arrived home twenty minutes earlier than usual. How long did he walk? (Mrs MacKeetch drives at a constant speed, and no time was lost in picking her husband up and turning round.)

56

Gaston and the Beer

* *

Many years ago during the famous monetary dis-
pute between Belgium and Luxemburg the Belgian
franc was worth only 90 centimes in Luxemburg
and the Luxemburg franc worth only 90 centimes
in Belgium. Gaston, a shrewd Belgian peasant, went
into a beer-hall in Luxemburg, bought a tankard
of beer for 10 centimes, paid for it with a Luxemburg franc, and requested his change in Belgian
money. He received one Belgian franc and returned
to the Belgian side of the border, where he visited a
similar beer-hall, bought beer for 10 centimes, and
received one Luxemburg franc in exchange after
having tendered his Belgian franc. He kept crossing
and re-crossing the border in this way all day long
until he had drunk as much beer as he could manage,
and when he finally returned to Belgium he still had
a full Belgian franc, which he had received in exchange during his final visit to the beer-hall in
Luxemburg. Who paid for Gaston's beer?

57
February 1972
* *

February 1972 has five Tuesdays. When was the last such February?

58
Arnold Toynbee's Grandfather
*

'In my case,' writes Arnold Toynbee in *Man's Concern with Death* (pp. 260–61), 'when I learned my name, I learnt at the same time the reason why I bore it. I learned that I had been called after an uncle of mine who had died six years before I had been born. I had been called after him because I had been the first male child in my uncle's and father's branch of the Toynbee family to be born after my uncle's death. . . . At the age of thirty [my uncle] had died, already a famous man. . . . On the day on which I am reading these words in proof, I myself am seventy-nine years and three months old. . . . Both my grandfathers had died prematurely and suddenly, though my Toynbee grandfather had lived to be twenty-one years older than his son Arnold was when Arnold died twenty-two years later than his father.'

How many years before Arnold Toynbee read his proofs was his grandfather born, and how many years intervened between the grandfather's death and the grandson's birth?

59

The Balloon

* *

Mr Tabako's little boy sits in the back seat of a closed motor-car, holding a balloon on a string. All the windows of the door are closed tight. The balloon is full of coal gas and is tethered by the string, which prevents it from touching the roof of the car. The car turns left at a roundabout. Does the balloon (a) swing left, (b) swing right, (c) stay upright, (d) do something else? And why?

(Given to me by Gerald Stonehill, Esq.)

60

Bombs

* *

On a station platform lie eleven piles of bombs, each pile consisting of exactly ten bombs. One pile consists entirely of miniature plutonium bombs, each weighing one pound; all the other piles contain only normal bombs, each weighing two pounds. All the bombs look identical, but you are in a desperate hurry to discover which are the plutonium bombs. You cannot risk trusting your own judgment by picking up the bombs and comparing their weights. Fortunately there is an accurate weighing machine on the platform; the attendant agrees that you may weigh any number of the 110 bombs, but insists that you use the weighing machine for only one single weighing operation. How do you use the weighing-machine to identify the pile of plutonium bombs?

61

Nobel Prizes

*

On the occasion of receiving his second Nobel Prize Dr Linus Pauling, the chemist, remarked that, while the chances of any person in the world receiving his first Nobel prize were one in several billion (the population of the world), the chances of receiving a second Nobel prize were one in several hundred (the total number of living people who had received the prize in the past) and that therefore it was less remarkable to receive one's second prize than one's first. In sixty seconds and the simplest possible language explain the fallacy (if any).

62

Transformations

* *

These transformations are by Lewis Carroll. Here is a simple example of how it is done: *cat* . . . cot . . . cog . . . *dog*. Now change the following:

(a) *hare* into *soup* in 7 steps,
(b) *black* into *white* in 8 steps,
(c) *army* into *navy* in 8 steps,
(d) *elm* into *oak* in 8 steps.

63

Longfellow's Bees

*

Henry Wadsworth Longfellow used to give this pretty puzzle to students of literature: if one fifth of a hive of bees flies to the ladamba flower, one third to the slandbara, three times the difference of these two numbers to an arbour, and one bee continues to fly about, attracted on each side by the fragrant ketaki and the malati, how many bees are there?

SOLUTIONS

SOLUTIONS

1

Father O'Sullivan is entirely correct. It is just as if two different monks set out along the same path at the same time and on the same day, one going up and the other going down. Whatever their relative speeds may be, they are bound to meet along the path. At that moment they will be in the same place and, by the very definition of the word 'meet', it will be the same time of the day for both of them.

2

The Chancellor divides the undergraduates into two groups, one consisting of 99 and the other of 1. He then addresses the following 1st question to any member of the larger group: 'If I were to ask you whether any member of your group is an equivocator (that is, someone who occasionally tells the truth and occasionally doesn't), would you answer yes?' If the answer is no, *he addresses the following 2nd question to one of the members of the larger group, but not to the student he first asked: 'If I were to ask you whether the recent drug traffic is controlled by the Mafia, would you* answer yes?' If the answer is yes, he knows that the Mafia is in control; if no, that it isn't. If the answer to the 1st question was yes, he asks the same 2nd question to the single undergraduate (i.e. the one in the smaller of the two groups), and the significance of the answer is the same as above. Alternatively the Chancellor's 1st question, addressed to any student A at random, could be: 'If I asked you whether student B was an equivocator, would you say yes?' If A answers yes, the Chancellor addresses his 2nd question (which is the same as in the earlier solution) to C; if A answers no, the 2nd question is addressed to B. In both solutions the aim of the 1st question is to 'eliminate' the equivocator, so that the 2nd question may be addressed to someone who is consistently truthful or dishonest.

3

MacKeetch's daughter is best. She and her twin brother were born in the same year as MacKeetch's sister, who is the worst player.

4

Tabako would have to travel at an infinite speed on the second lap. If he averaged 60 m.p.h. for two laps, *they would take precisely two minutes; and the two minutes have already been used up in the first lap at 30 m.p.h.*

5

She puts one cultured pearl in jar A and all the other pearls in jar B. Then the chances of picking a cultured pearl from jar A are 99/99 and the chances of picking one from jar B are 49/99. Cumulatively the chances of picking a cultured pearl are the average of these two figures, viz. 74 to 25.

Supplementary: *To produce the least possible chance she would put one natural pearl in one jar and all the other pearls in the other jar: the chances of picking a cultured pearl at random would then be 25 in 99.*

6

There are many ways of combining these premises, but all lead to the same ineluctable conclusion: Prunella van Blitz has a chance of becoming a creative artist of no mean stature.

7

To prove: BLACK ≠ √BEAUTIFUL or BLACK² ≠ BEAUTIFUL. (i) B must be 1, (ii) therefore L must be 0, 2, 3, or 4, (iii) but, since K² ends in L, L≠ 0, 2, or 3, (iv) so L = 4; (v) therefore E = 9 and (vi) A = 6, 7, or 8; (vii) therefore BLACK > 14,600, (viii) therefore BLACK² > 199,999,999 ≠ B........ (Q.E.D.)

8

T. H. O'Beirne gives the following neat solution (capital letters denote husbands and the corresponding small letters denote their wives):

	near bank		in the boat		far bank
(i)	ABC abc		*none*		*none*
(ii)	AC ac	⟶	B b ⟶		*none*
(iii)	AC ac	⟵	B	⟵	b
(iv)	ABC	⟶	ac	⟶	b
(v)	ABC	⟵	a	⟵	bc
(vi)	A a	⟶	BC ⟶		bc
(vii)	A a	⟵	B b ⟵		C c
(viii)	ab	⟶	AB ⟶		C c
(ix)	ab	⟵	c	⟵	ABC
(x)	b	⟶	ac	⟶	ABC
(xi)	b	⟵	B	⟵	AC ac

| (xii) none | B b $\longrightarrow$ | AC ac |
| (xiii) none | none | ABC abc |

9

The smallest possible number is 3,121, in which case the numbers left after each of the men has finished dealing with the pile are 2,496 . . . 1,996 . . . 1,596 . . . 1,276 . . . 1,020. In the final division each man receives 204 coco-nuts. As in most difficult puzzles, the best approach is to simplify the details and then clarify the underlying principles. In the puzzle as stated there were five successive removals of coco-nuts. Let us suppose that there was only one such removal. Then, if y is the final number of coco-nuts and x the original number, $y = x - 1 - \dfrac{x-1}{5}$ and $4x = 5y + 4$. Since y must be divisible by 5, the lowest integer it can represent (if x is also to be an integer) is obviously 20, and x is then 26 (check: $26 - 1 - 5 = 20$). By the same logic the formula for five removals is therefore $1024a - 8404 = 3125y$ where a is the original number of coco-nuts. The only numbers that fit this equation if y is to be divisible by 5 are 3121 and 1020.

Supplementary: *15,621. (The series is 15,621 . . . 12,496 . . . 9,996 . . . 7,996 . . . 6,396 . . . 5,116.)*

10

For some reason that I do not understand 4 is the maximum number needed for any known number of divisions.

11

The most efficient solution I have seen is that suggested by Lady Violet Powell as follows: (i) 10–0–0, (ii) 7–3–0, (iii) 7–0–3, (iv) 4–3–3, (v) 4–5–1, (vi) 4–0–1, (vii) 4–1–0, (viii) 1–1–3, (ix) 1–1–0, (x) 0–1–1. Gaston drinks a total of 8 litres in steps v and viii; as will be obvious from puzzle no. 56, he has a large capacity for beer.

12

645 relations.

7 married couples	14
3 widows	3
12 bachelors	12
10 girls	10
	——
	39 people

If every one of these 39 had relations once with everyone else, the number of relations would be 741 (39 × 19); and, if the 12 bachelors had relations with the 10 girls once again, we add 120, making 861. But as no married man made love to a married woman other than his own wife, we deduct 42; as no male homosexual relations took place, we deduct 171; as no widow had relations with another widow, we deduct a further 3. The answer is therefore 861 − 42 − 171 − 3 = 645.

Supplementary: *The unmarried girls were the most active: each had fifty encounters during the month.*

13

The conclusion, which is correct and needs no further premise, tells us that Suzuki is unkind by nature. The premises can be combined as follows: (i) if some Japanese (e.g. Suzuki) are tall and tall people are inscrutable, then some Japanese are inscrutable; (ii) if all generous people are scrutable, and some Japanese are inscrutable, then some Japanese are not generous; (iii) if honest people are generous and some Japanese not generous, then some Japanese are dishonest; (iv) if kind people are always honest and some Japanese dishonest, then some Japanese (including tall, inscrutable, ungenerous, dishonest Professor Suzuki) are unkind.

14

It is a slim (but exquisite) volume of five pages, and it will take him 114 days and 4 hours to complete. We know that during the first ten days his speed is $\frac{1}{10}$ of a page daily and that during the last fifty days it has fallen to $\frac{1}{50}$ of a page daily. Since he writes $\frac{1}{50}$ of a page daily when he has one page left to write, it appears that his daily speed of writing is $\frac{1}{50}$ of the number of remaining pages. So, if $\frac{1}{10}$ of a page is $\frac{1}{50}$ of the total number of pages, the book must be $\frac{50}{10} = 5$ pages long—a slim volume indeed. Therefore the first page took 10 days, the second page $12\frac{1}{2}$ days, the third page $16\frac{2}{3}$ days, the fourth page 25 days, and the fifth page 50 days—a total of $114\frac{1}{6}$ days (not necessarily at a stretch).

15

Fifty. Again the easiest method is to reduce the number and simplify the variables. Let us suppose that he saw four cars when in motion and the journey from Kyoto to Bingo took one hour. Then it is clear that, if he remained stationary at Kyoto for one hour, he would see only two of the four cars that he saw when moving; by the time the third car reached Kyoto the hour would have elapsed.

16

July 1958. The youngest child was born in February 1968; the two oldest children must therefore have been born in January 1956 and July 1958, January–July being the only pair of months that satisfies the stated conditions. After the birthday of the second child in July until the birthday of the first child in January it sounds as if there were an interval of two years between the ages of these two children if only the years of birth are mentioned, whereas in fact there is a difference of two and a half years.

17

(a) no e's;

(b) all words begin with consonants;

(c) all nouns and verbs are modified by adjectives and adverbs;

(f) e's in every word.

(d) they all begin with vowels.

(e) none are so modified.

18

Opinions differ about the solution. I believe that Algernon must be correct. He knows from the outset that Basil and/or Cyril will die, and the gaoler's information makes no difference to his own chances. The gaoler's reference to 'your chances of survival as you see them' is meaningless. As Mr Lawrence Latto points out, 'his chances are whatever they are, and, if he happens to believe that they are not what they are, this does not serve to change them' (a telling commentary on the human condition in general). By far the strongest argument in support of the gaoler's point of view has been expressed by Professor Arthur Danto as follows: 'Originally there were three possible combinations of execution (AB, AC, BC) and two of these included Algernon. But once Algernon knows that Basil is definitely going to be executed there are only two possible combinations (AB and BC), of which one includes him. This fits a standard interpretation of probability as a function of evidence. The evidence is changed since the reference class is changed. Before, the reference class was Algernon, Basil, and Cyril; now the reference class has been narrowed to just Algernon and Cyril.' Dr Harry Hazard has provided the following rebuttal, which incidentally explains the answer to the supplementary: 'Before asking his question, Alger-

non knew that three combinations were equally likely:
AB, AC, and BC. If he persuades the gaoler to specify,
and the latter eliminates AC, this does not change the
1/3 probability of AB to 1/2 but to 2/3. If A is
scheduled to live, the gaoler might equally answer "B"
or "C"; if B is scheduled to live, he would not answer
"B"; if C is scheduled to live, he must answer "B".
So a B answer is twice as likely to mean AB (when
it is forced) as BC (when it is a 50–50 option), and
thus AB acquires all of AC's probability, leaving BC
unchanged. A knows that one solution is barred, but
that does not make the other two equally likely.'
Hazard suggests this analogy: a bag holds a red ball, a
white ball, and a black ball. Replacing the red ball by a
second black ball or vice versa (= if the gaoler had
answered 'C') does not improve the chances of drawing
a white ball, which remain 1 in 3.

Supplementary: *Cyril's correct conclusion will be that*
he now has a two-thirds chance of survival while
Algernon's chances remain at one-third.

19

(a) artichoke; (b) lift in an ocean liner; (c) pearl
oyster.

20

L.

21

Yes, he is mistaken. The coin is irrelevant; what matters is the amount they originally paid for the barrel. This expense would normally have been redeemed by the customers' purchases; now it won't be.

22

*If ☷ is 1, it would appear that an unbroken line on top is equivalent to 1 and a broken line means 0. Then, since ☳ is 3, it appears that an unbroken line in the middle is 2. Evidently the value of the unbroken line doubles as its position is lowered. We might therefore expect its value in the bottom position to be 4, and since ☵ is 6, this expectation must be correct. ☶ is therefore equivalent to 4. As Arthur Waley points out (*Madly Singing in the Mountains: An Appreciation and Anthology of Arthur Waley, *edited by Ivan Morris, Allen & Unwin, 1970), Leibniz recognized some two centuries ago that the Eight Diagrams* *of Fu Hsi were in fact the numbers 0–7 written in a binary notation.*

23

(a) *Only* intransigent *has no affirmative form; tolerant, pervious, peccable, trepid, and hospitable are all in the unabridged dictionary.*

(b) *donate, gotten, kilter, railroaded, tenderloin, pursue. Only* pursue *is not now regarded as 'originally or chiefly American'.*

(c) *passtime, allign, forsee, descend, pavillion, stupour. Only* descend *is spelt correctly.*

24

(a) *If he had only known that—that that that that girl said was true—he would have avoided much sorrow.*

(b) *On examining the sign carefully, I noticed that the spacings between 'Goat' and 'and' and 'and' and 'Compass' were unequal. (Solution suggested by E. Armitage, Esq.)*

(c) *Nahum, where Malachi had had 'had had', had had 'had'; 'had had' had had the examiners' approval.*

25

1st way: 1 cubed plus 12 cubed;
2nd way: 9 cubed plus 10 cubed.

26

(a) *MacGregor is a dwarf and cannot reach higher than the button for the 25th floor.*

(b) *The man was snoring.*

27

(a) *Not more than 4 questions will be necessary, but sometimes (in one case out of three) 3 questions will suffice.*

1st question *(addressed to the 1st banker): 'If I asked you whether the 2nd banker is an equivocator (i.e. a person who sometimes tells lies and sometimes tells the truth), would you say yes?' If he answers yes, we know that the 3rd banker cannot possibly be an equivocator and we accordingly address our subsequent questions to him; if the 1st banker answers no, we know that the 2nd banker is not an equivocator and we ask him our subsequent questions.*

2nd question *(addressed to the 3rd or 2nd banker depending on whether the answer to the 1st question was yes or no respectively)*: '*If I asked you whether the 1st banker is Albanian, would you answer yes?*' If the answer is yes, the 3rd question *(asked to the same person as the 2nd question)* is: '*If I asked you whether the 2nd banker is American, would you say yes?*' By elimination we now know the identity of the 3rd banker also. If, on the other hand, the answer to the 2nd question is no, two further questions will be required *(a total of 4)*. 3rd question: '*If I asked you whether the 1st banker is American, would you say yes?*' If the answer is yes, we know that the 1st banker is American; if it is no, we know that he is Austrian. In either case we require one further question *(the 4th question)* to identify the two remaining bankers. Since the 1st question '*eliminates*' the equivocator, we know that the remaining questions are addressed to someone who is consistently honest or consistently dishonest; and the questions are so worded that the answers will be the same whether he is honest or dishonest. The moral is that consistently dishonest people are far more dependable than those who occasionally tell the truth.

*(b) An infinite number of questions would be needed to find out the nationality of the fishermen since it is impossible in any finite number of questions to '*eliminate*' the equivocator.*

White plays P× BP (en passant) *and his next move is P–B7 (mate). This is simple enough, but why is the seeming alternative (viz. P× QP (e.p.) and P–Q7 (mate)) not possible? Here is my full analysis: (a) White's pawns cannot have got into their present bizarre positions without having made at least 10 captures; (b) since Black has only 6 pieces left, all his other pieces, including his Queen's Bishop, must therefore have been captured by pawns; (c) his Queen's Bishop must have been captured on some square other than its QB1, else the capturing White pawn would have been promoted (this is compulsory) and White would not have his full complement of pawns; (d) his Queen's Bishop must therefore have moved from QB1; (e) it could not have moved on the N2–R3 diagonal since this has been blocked from the beginning of the game; (f) therefore it must have moved on the Q2– K3 diagonal; (g) therefore Black's Queen's Pawn must have moved at some time in the game prior to the last move; (h) therefore, if White is to mate in two moves, Black's last move must have been P–KB4; (i) therefore White must play P× BP e.p., followed by P–B7 mate.*

29

2, 2, 9.   There are eight groups of three numbers whose products are 36. Of the eight associated sums only one is duplicated: 13. This must be the house number of Professor Baba because with any other house number he would have had enough information after the initial statement by Suzuki. The other group of 3 numbers is 1, 6, 6 where of course no one is the oldest child to 'look exactly like me'.

30

(a)

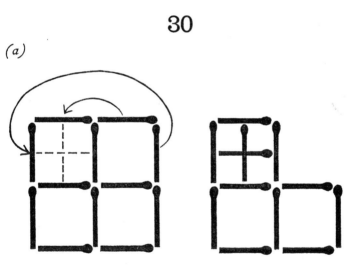

31

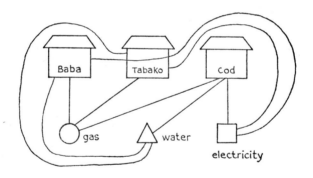

The real difficulty occurs if Baba, Tabako, and Cod all refuse to allow a pipe to pass through their houses on its way to one of their neighbours. In fact it is not merely

difficult; it is impossible. H. E. Dudeney proves this impossibility in the following ingenious way: assume that only two houses, A and B, are to be supplied. The relative positions of the various buildings clearly make no difference whatever. These figures show two positions for the two houses:

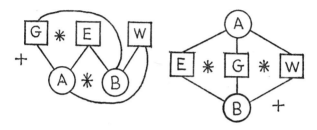

Wherever you build these houses the effect will be the same—one of the supply stations will be cut off. In these examples it will be seen that if you build a third house on the outside (say in the position indicated by one of the black crosses) the gas can never reach you without crossing a pipe. Whereas if you put the house inside one of the enclosures (as indicated by the stars) then you must be cut off either from the water or from the electricity—one or the other. Therefore a position is impossible in which it can be supplied from all three stations without one pipe crossing another (or passing through another house).

Alfonso's chances are 5/12, Bertram's 3/12, and Casimir's 4/12. Alfonso's best strategy is to fire his first shot in the air. Bertram will then fire at Casimir. He has 1 chance in 2 of killing him; if he fails, Casimir will fire at Bertram and infallibly kill him. On his second round Alfonso therefore has equal chances of being confronted with Bertram or Casimir, and this time he must shoot to kill. If his adversary is Casimir his chances of surviving the round are 1/3; if it is Bertram, his chances are 1/2. The reason that, if A and B survive to shoot it out, with A having the first shot, A's chances of survival are 1/2 can be explained as follows: for each round there are three equally likely solutions: (α) A kills B (1 in 3), (β) A misses B (2 in 3), and B kills A (1 in 2, for a combined chance of 1 in 3), and (γ) A misses B (2 in 3) and B misses A (likewise 1 in 2, for a combined chance of 1 in 3), in which case the whole thing starts again. The chances that both A and B will survive x rounds is $\dfrac{1}{3^x}$; if x is infinitely large, the chances are infinitesimal, but if they are limited to a specified finite number, it is calculable; nevertheless A's and B's chances are always equal, approaching a limit of 1 in 2. A's cumulative chances *of surviving the entire ordeal are* $\dfrac{1/3 + 1/2}{2} = 5/12.$

(If, instead of firing his first shot in the air, Alfonso fires at Casimir, his chances of killing him are 1/3. Should he succeed, Bertram will fire his first shot at Alfonso (instead of at Casimir, as in the best arrangement) and the chances are then 1/2 that Alfonso will never have a chance to fire a second shot. If he fires his first shot at Bertram, his chances of ever firing a second shot become still smaller.)

On his first shot Bertram has a 50–50 chance of killing Casimir. If he fails, his chances of surviving the first round are nil; if he succeeds, he will have to shoot it out with Alfonso (Alfonso having the first shot) and his chances of survival are then 1/2 (as explained above). His cumulative chances of survival are therefore 1/2 × 2 = 1/4 = 3/12. If Casimir survives Bertram's first shot (his chances being 50–50), he will kill Bertram on his own first shot. Then he will shoot it out with Alfonso (Alfonso having the first shot) and his chances of survival will be 2/3. So his cumulative chances are $\dfrac{0 + 2/3}{2} = 2/6 = 4/12.$ *Dr Hazard notes a pleasing irony in the fact that the worst shot has the best chance of survival, but only if he fires in the air.*

Supplementary: *I do not know; readers are invited to*

send me their solutions in care of the publisher of this book.

33

361 (19 square). He gives 36 trees (i.e. 6 square) to each of the ten priests and is left with one for himself. The formula is $x^2 - 1 = ay^2$ where a is the number of poor priests, x the number of rows in the original orchard, and y the number of rows in each of the new orchards. If a is 2, 6, 10, 12, 14, 15, etc., the equation can easily be solved by trial and error; but for 7, 13, and certain other numbers it is quicker to use the system of recurrent continued fractions (if one happens to know it).

Supplementary *421,201 trees (649 square).*

34

Three people. This can be worked out by common sense and a little patience; but for those who like a formula that will apply to any number of picks (a) and any number of things to choose from (b) the following (provided by Lawrence Latto, Esq.) will be profitable:

$$1 - \left[\frac{(b-1)!}{b^{(a-1)} \times (b-a)!}\right].$$

Professor Baba's chances of winning if there were two people in the room were one in four; with three people they are five in eight.

35

Here is a partial list: aphidian, arachnoid, asinine #, avian, batrachian, batty #, bitchy #, bovine #, (canine,) (capricious #,) catty #, cetacean, chelonean, (cocky #,) coltish, colubrine, crabby #, currish #, dogged, elephantine #, equine, feline #, feral, fishy #, foxy #, halcyon, hircine, ichthyoid, kittenish, leonine, (lousy #,) mammoth, mousy #, (mulish #,) ovine #, owlish #, pithecoid, porcine #, psittacine, ratty #, saurian #, scalloped, sheepish #, simian #, slothful #, sluggish #, spidery #, swinish #, taurine, vermicular, vulpine #, waspish #. As will be seen, most of these words (the ones marked #) refer to negative or unpleasant characteristics; a few are neutral or ambiguous; hardly any are favourable. The same applies to verbs of the type: to dog, parrot, bitch, monkey with; and to nouns of the type: goose, popinjay, peacock, shrew. Mr Ivor Brown, to whom I described my Fifteen Minute Word Game, comments: 'Would bitchy pass? It is frequently used of and by young women in their impolite conversation. But if an M.P. complained in the House that one of his female colleagues had made a bitchy attack on the Minister what would Mr Speaker say? He might ask the hon. gentleman not to be currish . . . What about owlish? I would take it to mean solemnly stupid, but the owl is also the symbol of wisdom. I suppose 'the quality shared' by such words is that they are usually unkind to animals, from asinine onwards. We are great dog-lovers but are very unkind to them in our choice of language. Why 'sick as a dog', never 'healthy as a dog', and 'dirty dog', never 'clean dog'?

36

The shortest route is 40 feet.
The course is different and the distance shorter than 'common sense' would suggest. This can be verified by constructing a simple three-dimensional model and

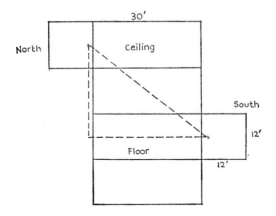

opening it up as above. The distance x that the scorpion must travel is the hypotenuse of the right-angled triangle of which the other two sides are (i) $6' + 12' + 6' = 24'$, (ii) $1' + 30' + 1' = 32'$. Since the square of the hypotenuse is the sum of the squares of the other two sides, $x^2 = 24^2 + 32^2 = 1600$, and $x = 40$.

37

There are 120 men. The equation is

$$\frac{2x}{3} + \frac{3x}{4} + \frac{4x}{5} - 2x = 26;$$

therefore $133x - 120x = 1560$ and $x = 120$.

AIR. This ingenious charade probably existed as early as 1841. I presented it to the readers of the Times Literary Supplement on 15th May 1969. My letter was followed by a lively, erudite, and inconclusive correspondence (T.L.S., 29.v.69, 5.vi.69, 19.vi.69, 3.vii.69, 7.viii.69). Among the many ingenious solutions were the following: AIR, FLAG, GOD, GUTS, HAM, MOLE, RA, SNAKE. By far the most convincing solution seemed to be that of Mrs Margaret Austen-Leigh of Isel Hall, Cockermouth, who gave AIR: 'Couplet 1. South wind (air in motion): gentle when calm; in tempest Euroclydon (or Sirocco), giving pun on rock; 2. East wind: monsoon, the break (or nod) which oriental kings in India, Siam, &c., watch for, that they may plant crops in wind-fertilized soil. 3. North wind: made visible by snow and ice; known only to a few polar explorers; bitter cold hated by all. 4. West wind: sent to Noah, sole remnant of humanity; controls flood; blowing one night and day, as Jewish legend states. 5. Atmospheric pressure (static air) is 3 lbs. per square inch, equivalent to a column of air a mile high. 6. South and West gales: trade winds; bring Gulf Stream. (As an alternative explanation of the 6th couplet Mrs

Austen-Leigh suggests Alexandra Regina 'who, as a beautiful queen, could have been said to be the Boast of Our Isle'. This of course will not work if the riddle dates back to 1841.) The final couplet, which is far inferior in quality to the rest of this beautifully worded riddle, serves to eliminate all solutions but AIR.

39

15 operations. Number the beetles from left to right: a, b, c, d, e, f; then (i) d moves left, (ii) c jumps right, (iii) b moves right (this is the move that most people miss at first), (iv) d jumps left, (v) d jumps left, (vi) e jumps left, (vii) e jumps left, (viii) b moves right, (ix) a jumps right, (x) c moves right, (xi) f jumps left, (xii) c moves right, (xiii) b jumps right, (xiv) f moves left, (xv) a jumps right.

40

(a) Eliot's, (b) denotes, (c) posts.

41

Each son rides the other son's horse.

42

*Seven. The only number into which 7 different numbers
of jelly-beans can be divided and produce the children's
ages is 180. The ages of the children must be 3, 4, 9,
10, 12, 15, and 18; and the numbers of beans that they
receive are respectively 60, 45, 20, 18, 15, 12, and 10.
Since Nonchan received 18 jelly-beans, she is 10 years
old; the youngest child is 3.*

43

(a) *If the grate be empty, put coal on; if the grate be
full, stop putting coal on.*

(b) *Au s——, au s——, au secours! Il m'encule dans
un coin.*

(c) *Tu entres peu. Tu entres trop. Arrêtes, arrêtes,
barbare!*

44

*Four. The economy involved in the principle of the
chess clock applies only when there are two players.*

45

20 m.p.h. The distance that the courier 'loses' on his way to the head of the moving column is precisely balanced by the distance that he 'gains' on his return journey.

46

There is absolutely no reason that the net amount paid by the three men plus the amount retained by the porter should equal the amount originally paid to the hotel. What we can expect is that the net amount paid by the three men equals the net amount received by the hotel plus the sum kept by the porter. And so it does: $(30-3) = (30-5)+2$.

47

(a) 1,236. It will be seen that the last digit in each of the 12 numbers is the last digit in the sum of the preceding digits (e.g. $8+0 = 8$, $7+6 = 13$, $4+9 = 13$). Let us then remove all these final digits. It will be found that the sum of the numbers in the outer circle (80, 83, 89, etc.) equals the

central number (450). If x leads to the missing number, the sum of the numbers in the second circle plus x will also equal the central number. Therefore 327+x = 450, and x = 123. To obtain the missing number we add together the digits of x (6) and append the final digit. So the missing number must be 1,236.

(b) They are the only numbers less than 100 which are the sum of 5 consecutive integers none of which is a perfect square. The next numbers in the series are 100, 105, and 110.

(c) 40. Each number is the cumulative sum of all odd prime numbers (1+3+5+7+11+13).

48

Suzuki owes Tabako 250 francs. The tip must have been 100 francs, since 500 is the only figure in the category of 'a few hundred' whose digits add up to five times the sum of the digits of its fifth (i.e. 1×5 = 5). Tabako therefore paid a total of 600 francs (500 for the bill plus 100 for the tip). Since the wine cost one third as much as the food, its price must have been 150 francs. Therefore Suzuki and Tabako each consumed 150 francs' worth of food and 50 francs' worth of wine. Mrs Tabako had no wine, but 150 francs' worth of food; Mrs Suzuki had no food but despite her diarrhoea drank 50 francs' worth of wine.

Supplementary: *A mental effort and deliberate decision are required for deciding the amount of the tip; not so for most bills.*

49

Percy's father must have been born in 1881. The property shared by 1881 and 1961 is that they read the same when turned upside down. The next year in this series is 6009. Percy will therefore have to live to the ripe old age of 4048.

50

(a) *facetious, abstemious.*
(b) *uncomplimentary (Dr H. W. Hazard), subcontinental (James Michie, Esq.), unnoticeably (Professor H. Webb).*

51

*The winner removes all 8 sticks from the largest pile.
This leaves the arrangement*

I   II   III   IIII   IIIII   IIIIII

*which is invincible if the winner continues to make the
correct removals. If, for example, the other player now
removes 1 stick from the 1-pile and 1 stick from the
3-pile (leaving 2-2-4-5-6), the winner simply removes
1 stick from the 5-pile and produces what is a winning
combination, 2-2-4-4-6. As in all the many variations
of Nim, the correct move can always be found by binary
breakdown of the numbers. In the basic game we
balance pairs (2-2, 4-4, 8-8, etc.); in this variation we
balance triplets (2-2-2, 4-4-4, 8-8-8, etc.). For a brief
explanation of the principle of Nim see Ivan Morris,*
The Pillow-Book Puzzles, *Bodley Head 1969,
p. 121; for a full analysis see T. H. O'Beirne,*
Puzzles and Paradoxes, *Oxford 1965, pp. 151–167.*

52

*If no Japanese is to sit next to a non-Japanese, the
Japanese will all have to sit along one side of the table,
and the two ends will be unoccupied; the Professor's*

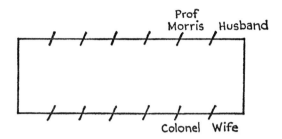

wife, who is obviously Japanese (since otherwise a Japanese could not sit next to her), must be at the end of the Japanese side next to the (Japanese) Colonel; her husband will sit opposite her at the end of the other side of the table next to Professor Morris, who must be a non-Japanese.

53

No. Though each of the sons gets more than was specified by their father's Will, and though the camels happily escape mutilation, the Will itself has been violated, because it provided that $\frac{17}{18}$ of a camel (i.e. 17 minus $\frac{17}{2}$ minus $\frac{17}{3}$ minus $\frac{17}{9}$) was to remain after the division between the sons. The Great Mosque (the residuary legatee) and anyone who believed that the terms of the Sheik's Will should be strictly observed would be dissatisfied with the wise man's arrangement.

54

(a) *10,652 (9,567 plus 1,085).*

(b) *4 million. This may seem difficult but it isn't. All observant people who do multiplication must have noticed that when 9 or a multiple of 9 is multiplied by any number the product is invariably a number whose digits add up to 9 or to a multiple of 9. Therefore the digits in the product of 27 and* a *will add up to a multiple of 9, and* b *must be 8. The rest is mechanical:* $\frac{108,000,000}{27} = 4$ *million.*

(c) *287× 39, 861× 13, 681× 17.*

55

Fifty minutes. Since Mr MacKeetch left 60 minutes earlier than usual and reached home only 20 minutes earlier, the journey took an extra 40 minutes, this being the difference between the walking-time and the driving-time from the station to the pick-up point; therefore the driving-time was 40 minutes less than the walking-time. Mrs MacKeetch drove 20 minutes less than usual; this represents the time normally taken between the station and the pick-up point and back, which must therefore be 10 minutes each way. Therefore the driving-time from the station to the pick-up point is 10 minutes. Therefore the walking-time is 50 minutes (40 + 10).

56

No, he did not pay for it himself by his own exertions. According to John Train, Esq., it was all the users (including Gaston himself) of Belgian and Luxemburg currency who paid for Gaston's drinks, since his series of transactions was bound to have an inflationary effect that slightly decreased the purchasing power of the franc in both countries. According to Dr Harry Hazard, however, those whose losses paid for Gaston's beer are the tourists who exchanged their currency in the opposite direction at unfavourable rates.

(Readers are invited to arbitrate on this fundamental economic disagreement.)

57

1944. Only leap-years have five Tuesdays (or five of any other day) in February. A five-Tuesday leap-year comes once every seven leap-years, i.e. once every 28 years.

58

The number of years between Professor Toynbee's reading of his proofs and his grandfather's death was 158·25 (= 79·25+6+22+30+21). The grandfather died 28 (6+22) years before the grandson was born.

59

Master Tabako's balloon swings left. This may seem peculiar, but it can easily be verified by acquiring a gas-filled balloon (and a car and a small child). The balloon is full of gas, which is lighter than air and therefore remains suspended at the top of the string. The situation in the motor-car therefore is completely analogous to a captive air bubble in a bottle of beer: if you swing the bottle of beer round you in a circle, the centrifugal force takes the liquid outwards and the air bubble goes towards the centre. By the same process, when the car goes round the roundabout the heavier mass of air will be drawn from the outside (right) of the roundabout and the balloon will lean towards the inside (left) of the roundabout.

60

Number the piles from a to k; take 1 bomb from pile b, 2 from pile c, 3 from pile d, etc., until you get to pile k, from which you take all bombs. Put these 55 bombs on the weighing machine. If the weight is 110 pounds, you know that all 55 bombs are normal and that therefore pile a consists of plutonium bombs. If the total weight is 109, pile b has the plutonium bombs; if the total weight is 108, pile c is plutonium, etc.

61

The chances that a previous recipient will receive a prize have been deliberately confused with the chances that any human being will receive a second prize. The fallacy is obvious but surprisingly hard to explain in a few simple words. I should be interested to hear some clearer and more succinct answers than mine.

62

(a) hare ... hark ... hack ... sack ... sock ... soak ... soap ... soup OR hare ... hale ... hall ... hail ... sail ... soil ... soul ... soup.

(b) black ... slack ... stack ... stalk ... stale ... shale ... whale ... while ... white OR black ... slack ... shack ... shark ... share ... shire ... shine ... whine ... white.

(c) army ... arms ... aims ... dims ... dams ...
    dame ... name ... nave ... navy.
(d) elm ... ell ... all ... ail ... air ... fir ... far
    ... oar ... oak. OR elm . alm . arm
    ark .. ork .. oak.

63

Fifteen bees.